Dear Parent:
Your child's love of reading starts here!

Every child learns to read in a different way and at his or her own speed. Some go back and forth between reading levels and read favorite books again and again. Others read through each level in order. You can help your young reader improve and become more confident by encouraging his or her own interests and abilities. From books your child reads with you to the first books he or she reads alone, there are I Can Read Books for every stage of reading:

SHARED READING
Basic language, word repetition, and whimsical illustrations, ideal for sharing with your emergent reader

BEGINNING READING
Short sentences, familiar words, and simple concepts for children eager to read on their own

READING WITH HELP
Engaging stories, longer sentences, and language play for developing readers

READING ALONE
Complex plots, challenging vocabulary, and high-interest topics for the independent reader

ADVANCED READING
Short paragraphs, chapters, and exciting themes for the perfect bridge to chapter books

I Can Read Books have introduced children to the joy of reading since 1957. Featuring award-winning authors and illustrators and a fabulous cast of beloved characters, I Can Read Books set the standard for beginning readers.

A lifetime of discovery begins with the magical words **"I Can Read!"**

Visit www.icanread.com for information
on enriching your child's reading experience.

To Meadow
—R.S.

I Can Read Book® is a trademark of HarperCollins Publishers.

Splat the Cat Makes Dad Glad
Copyright © 2014 by Rob Scotton
All rights reserved. Manufactured in China.
No part of this book may be used or reproduced in any manner whatsoever without written permission except in the case of brief quotations embodied in critical articles and reviews. For information address HarperCollins Children's Books, a division of HarperCollins Publishers, 195 Broadway, New York, NY 10007.
www.icanread.com

Library of Congress catalog card number: 2013956398
ISBN 978-0-06-211599-7 (trade bdg.) —ISBN 978-0-06-211597-3 (pbk.)

16 17 18 19 SCP 10 9 8 7 6   ❖   First Edition

I Can Read!

BEGINNING 1 READING

Splat the Cat

Makes Dad Glad

Based on the bestselling books by Rob Scotton

Cover art by Rick Farley

Text by Alissa Heyman

Interior illustrations by Robert Eberz

HARPER

An Imprint of HarperCollinsPublishers

On Sunday morning,

Splat ate his favorite food, Fish Fad,

and read Super Cat comics.

Splat felt really glad!

Then Splat's dad sat down
with a small frown.
"What's wrong, Dad?" asked Splat.
"Our soccer team
lost our big game last night,
and I'm a tad sad," said his dad.

"OH NO!" cried Splat.

He thought his dad

must be feeling very bad.

Splat's dad loved soccer.

He was the captain of his team.

"I have to cheer up Dad!

I think he's feeling really sad.

I'll find out what makes him glad

by looking at old photos.

Look at this, Seymour!"

"It's Dad and Granddad
winning the three-legged race
when Dad was just a lad!"

"I know just what to do
to make Dad glad.
I'll sign us up for
Cat School Game Day.
We'll play lots of games,
and we'll win the three-legged race!"

"I'll make Dad proud.

I'll show him

I'm quick and strong,

just like he and Granddad were!"

"Splat, what are you doing?"

Little Sis asked.

"I have a brilliant plan

to make Dad glad!

And I'll practice with Seymour,"

cried Splat.

"Hmmm," said Little Sis.

"Your plan isn't half bad."

"What could possibly go wrong?"

said Splat, as he ran.

"Oops!" said Splat, landing with a thump.

His tail knotted up with worry,

but he put on a brave face.

"I know what to do.

I'll wear my lucky shoelace!"

The big day finally came,
and Splat felt really glad!
He and Seymour had practiced
the three-legged race every day.

The field behind Cat School
was crowded with cats of all ages.
Kitten was there and so was Plank.
And of course, Spike was there, too.

Spike strutted over to Splat

and grinned a big, toothy grin.

"I can't wait for the games to begin.

My mom and I are going to win, win, win!"

Splat's whiskers wilted just a bit.

"My dad and I are going to win

the three-legged race," said Splat.

"I've been practicing,

and I'm wearing my lucky shoelace!"

"No way, Splat!" sneered Spike.

"A coach helped us train for the race.

All you have is one lucky shoelace!"

First came the wheelbarrow race.

Yay! Splat and his dad were ahead.

And then they weren't.

"Owww!" Splat howled.

"I have a thorn in my paw pad."

Splat said, "I'm sorry, Dad."

"That's okay, son," Splat's dad replied.

"I'm just glad you weren't hurt."

But Splat wondered if his dad

might be a tad mad.

"Don't worry, Dad," said Splat.

"We still have the three-legged race,

and we won't lose that.

Now we have the egg toss."

Eggs started to fly
as Splat and his dad
lined up for the egg toss.
Splat caught his dad's egg
and smiled.

Splat tossed the egg back.

It was the perfect throw.

Oops! Another egg was headed

straight for his dad.

"Look out!" yelled Splat.

His dad looked up in surprise,
and two eggs hit him at once.
Egg yolk ran down his shirt.
Splat's dad did not look glad.
"It's okay, Dad," said Splat.
"There's still the big race!"

Finally, it was time

for the three-legged race.

"Get ready! Get set! Go!"

Splat's teacher, Mrs. Wimpydimple,

blew the whistle.

Off Splat went with his dad.

The pair passed Plank.

They passed Kitten.

They even passed Spike.

They were far in the lead,

when Splat felt something go wrong. . . .

Splat's lucky shoelace had come untied!

Splat went rolling. So did his dad.

They went tumbling, tumbling

down the hill, until SPLAT!

Splat and his dad fell

with a splash into a pond.

They sputtered and spat,

they floundered and splashed.

Finally, they were able to stand up,

covered from head to paw in lily pads.

"I'm so sorry, Dad.

I made you soggy and mad."

Then Splat stared at his dad.

His dad wasn't mad.

His dad was laughing!

"Splat, I'm not mad!"

"But you and Granddad won a trophy,
and we came in last," said Splat.

"I don't care about winning.
This is the most fun I've ever had!"

"Yippee!" said Splat.

"I did it! I made my dad glad!"